Table of Contents

Introduction

It was a surprise to me when I looked into my tanka notebook for 2008 (I always keep a yearly notebook on all the decades I have been writing tanka). What I discovered in the notebook for 2008 was that I had written a great many minimalist poems. I had read some minimalist writers, especially Raymond Carver, but as far as I know, I took no notes, and at 88 my memory is weak.

So why these minimalist poems? I have been told by my editor M. Kei that over the years I wrote many minimalist poems, so obviously I was attracted to the form. Why was that?

If we look back at the two kinds of tanka forms over the past decades, we see a definite pattern of 5-7-5-7-7—the thirty-one syllable format. I discovered years ago a new pattern of short-long-short-long-long. Of course the Japanese term "ji-amari" means that we can have, for example, 8 or 9 syllables in the last line or 6 syllables in a first line, that is to say more syllables than the standard form requires or even a shorter length. This does not happen often. What happens when we are writing a traditional tanka or one with longer and shorter lines is that the concentration is broken, for we are trying for a 5 or 7 syllable line. The same is true for short-long-short-long-long, a recent adoption which I have liked more than the 31-syllable form. We are always aware that we need syllables or have too many or want to settle for a longer line. So while we are writing a tanka, the concentration is limited, changes appear quite frequently, and sometimes we find we have to start over. In other words, something happened to the original feeling we had.

A minimalist poem gets its immediacy and we write it down. Often that is the way it is—an image, an event, a memory, a poem with an immediacy that does not require juggling. Of course there are times when we want to change a word or line, but the immediacy is still there.

I did not take notes on Richard Carver, a major minimalist short story writer and novelist, but he himself did not like the term. On the Internet I found him saying that if he revised a story of 20 pages, it often became 60. No, minimalism is a state of mind. Something appears in the mind and before one realizes it, the poem has been formed. Of course it may be revised or rewritten at times, but the core of the image remains. And still I think spontaneity is the major clue. That is how I think the process works.

And so these minimalist poems that exploded in my 2008 tanka notebook or exploded at other times were spontaneous. I was not planning to publish them and was surprised to find so many. This must be what is behind most of the minimalist poems.

I did borrow certain subjects from some of the articles I read, but each poem comes from something in my experience, in my feelings, in my memory, in my past or future. I offer these to my readers in what may perhaps be my last book, though I said that about my previous book published in 2013, *Journeys Far and Near: tanka roads*, but here I am again, with thanks to my magnificent editor M. Kei and to my artist friend Kazuaki Wakui. I do thank Kim Herzinger for some topics she considered part of Minimalism.

Sanford Goldstein
New Year's Eve
December 31, 2013

Kids

Sanford Goldstein

sudden
this thought of
my campus kid,
over-the-sea
with so much freedom

last night
chocolate
with almonds
before the set
with my end-of-exam kid and me

.

I walk
my kid
to her weekend sojourn
I start back home
alone

This Short Life

his uncle
pleads to the kids,
bear up, bear up,
like your father
your mother

others find
some kid's glove
along a street,
sometimes by the cake window,
sometimes in a dog's dung

fluttering
those strips
of paper,
I see the child's casket.
Namu Amida Butsu*

　　　　　　　　　*save us merciful Buddha

Sanford Goldstein

like kids
we buy
a Sunday treat,
we devour it
before the set

my kid's letter
ending on a note
of worry,
the boy at the party
disappeared

my kid's face
tearful,
bereaved,
another history answer
gets a thumb's down

This Short Life

my kid
carrying it
home,
her lopsided
heart

going off
with her adopted
aunt,
my kid
never looks back

how short
my son's
miss you,
at the close of
today's letter

Sanford Goldstein

I leave
my kid
puzzled
under the colored
umbrella

my kid
on stage
singing Italian,
my lips
are parched

my kid
packs too,
off to her Japanese aunt,
me? heading
for Tokyo

This Short Life

two
of my kids
overseas,
my wife's ashes
in a Lafayette attic

all day
my fear
of rebuke,
what it might do
to my sensitive kid

the joyous
suspense
of my kid,
she asks me
to guess her history grade

I'm ready
to marry her
off,
my kid's first
baked dish

my kid
asks for a summer apartment
and braces,
she puts
the bite on me

my kid
tells me
to stay out,
she's tonight's
cook

This Short Life

my kid
dreams
of her own apartment,
her every minute
of her own day

my kids
play or cry
in the hospital
compound,
their mother's nearing the end

my kid's
onions
superior to mine,
how white
her kitchen apron

Sanford Goldstein

how long
my kid's face
in its desire
to turn off
those temporary pages

again
the diet's
off
and me and my kid
gorge before the set

up with the sun
my kid
with chores to do,
she curls her hair
for the new term

This Short Life

contented
she combs
her brown hair,
reminding me
a boy called her cute

closer
to my kid's
twenty-three-year-old face,
I picture myself
an ancient ham

my son heaps
bowl on bowl
with rice,
head-down
he devours the world

Minimalist Sexuality

Sanford Goldstein

still
he finds
translatable streets,
heroes twist and turn
on the spit of desire

what good's
self-touching
at night?
give me delirium
through this midnight mind

arousal
from a brief
street-moment,
up a stairway
and the mediocre returns

This Short Life

alone
with the usual equipment,
I give up,
before bed
I shower

I spit
on tonight's
lonely maneuver,
I floss,
I scribble poems

left
without will
to penetrate
that desired
space

Sanford Goldstein

naked
in front of
two mirrors,
I recall long-ago
impossibilities

how silent
that corner of flesh,
that hidden space,
I should have had
a pair of ragged claws

at least
in letters
she wanted it—
that evening
brittle, chewed

No

This Short Life

life drags
desire
with its winks,
its pokes,
its endless follow-after

the desire
can't be shed
with ease,
he looks up at the cold
February moon

from depths
something breaks
to tell him —
tonight's possibilities
lag

Sanford Goldstein

he avoided
the chances
he could have taken:
if he hadn't, his lusting
would not have been so puerile

I was
some unadorned corner,
not for beauty,
not for truth,
windows opened and closed

all these legs
and arms
and eyes,
all searching,
all wanting

This Short Life

almost
forty years ago
under neon,
was I too
wrapped in desire?

something
in this April light
tells me
this celibacy
will last and last

a beer bottle
dance
they called it,
the primitive un-self-consciousness
of the race

Sanford Goldstein

how easy
the slide into
that missing of desire,
he sees foreigners
in twos

Nature

take this hat,
wind,
at your risk—
I press down hard
to skull

it's a winter
of cuddling up
against heaters,
against socks,
against the prick of wool

a wind
that wanted
more,
this hat, this bundle,
this shopping bag

This Short Life

the rain
and winter chill
on these cold hands,
I cut salads
in this small kitchen

wanting
to fold
this self,
the paper crane
should be blue

a spring shower
over
the bridge,
a white pair
of wings

Sanford Goldstein

winds
of this February
bridge,
leave my brown hat
for this balding pate

asked if I like
Japanese calligraphy,
and I remember,
how splendid
the brush for bamboo!

the office heater
flame
and its softness,
outside there's pine
and the huddling of students

This Short Life

freezing
again
at the bus stop,
this February 11 p.m.
chill

the Chinese tea
warms,
settles,
outside,
a quiet snow

fog
shows the outline
of form—
I want something skeletal
this Thanksgiving day

Sanford Goldstein

to lie
pillow-bunched
by my ear,
I shut out
this rough November world

in the distance
snow ridges
beyond rice-less fields,
I'm Tokyo bound
trying to unwind

imagining
Ono and Lennon
strolling,
how natural
these park-walkers

This Short Life

only
to the lighthouse
and back,
this April morning's
seven-mile walk

I hold
this moving
line,
I wait
for seaside sound

after the wake,
his garden blossoms
and desire grows—
to live
live!

Sanford Goldstein

around
a pile
of flowers,
a wealth of vegetation
beyond his mother's casket face

looking
at pine needles
on the walk home,
I find they too
turn brown

this phoned
relief
along a seaside road,
may this dim April sunlight,
make me a call

This Short Life

want
something poetic
in nature?
I have only
these five lines down

they laugh
at this winter-coat
me —
it's April
and those kids bathing

trap me
a moon
above the brown-needled pine,
paint on one side a wild goose,
on the other, a three-dimensional worm

Sanford Goldstein

was it my dangling arm
looking like a pole
to that stray,
lifting its leg
and letting it pour down?

hard
to spill one
on this seaside curve—
look!
Sado Island distant in the haze

the March wind
cold, cold
and
cold too
these five lines down

This Short Life

pen
in hand
on a seaside bench,
time to record
a stone shadow

wave sounds
against these Sea of Japan
tetrahedrons,
loud to me this April morning,
April is the cruelest month

put
my sad now
out to dry,
how white
this April sky-light

Sanford Goldstein

to leap
through the tangle
so appealing!
and still it's only
an ordinary walk-along

the melody's
inward,
quiet,
April morning
and I walk to my morning class

is it remembrance
before bed,
this singing in the shower?
songs the dead one liked
on a winter night

This Short Life

I want to push
these lines out,
out,
out into this October light
to the very edge!

the cat
like something
out of Noh,
so delicate its footsteps
in an autumn field

sudden
as if from behind
a magician's cloth,
winter's
radiant snow

Sanford Goldstein

age
thickly sprawled
on a bus station bench,
she is waiting
for spring

I pass
the same
walk-along,
the same sudden cry
of a huge crow

a pink stretch
across the early
evening sky,
I have walked
ten miles today

This Short Life

I leap
into my brother's mind
across continents,
I pour the Pacific
into a vase of sad flowers

the rains
of early November
dampen my hat,
how quiet my pen
at the coffee shop

the bus window
steams
from rain and snow,
I try to ease my breaths
I count my zen life

no snowmen
in school parks,
in city gardens,
a sudden nostalgia
for nature's ease

seaside walk
and the vastness
of water,
enormous too
the length of shore waves

cramming
a fall universe
into five lines down,
pen in hand,
the seaside bench hard

This Short Life

the sad
small voices
of my distant kids,
they ask for a winter photograph
to confirm my existence

a seaside
morning with
pine shadows,
waves
responding to wind

not just
mere
winter description
oh, a minimalist depth
is what I want

Sanford Goldstein

take down
these mirrors
or cover them,
I've seen enough
of this winter face

how self-possessed
these winter
Japanese,
their shoes polished,
their necktie knots tight and neat

49

Cleanliness, Whiteness,
Purity

Sanford Goldstein

a morning
of real cleaning
with cold white socks,
from room to room
February's begun

how white
the water
last night,
how quiet the Italian
restaurant

under
my 11 p.m.
shower,
the white soap streaks
reciting my list of the dead

This Short Life

I swing
my heavy
bookbag,
how light
the February snow

tomorrow
the dusting,
the vacuuming,
another
Sunday morning

making
faces in the mirror
as I dust,
the usual Sunday
cleaning

Sanford Goldstein

sometimes
an exuberant
walk,
flinging confidence back
to this caved-in self

the Zen light
did not leave with
Long Sleeve's departure,
I sweep
I dust

as careful
as Christ's
washing,
the feet of that
Buddhist monk

This Short Life

no wax
on those temple floors,
only the daily rub-down,
a rub-down
with damp cloths

how we imagine
terrors turning
more grim,
often it turns
to pure laughter

to have
the freedom
of the full response,
today's milk-drinking
thought

Sanford Goldstein

my colleague
invites me in
for tea,
wordless,
we lift the white bowls

I lean
back in comfort
on the reserved seat,
and still
the quiet reserve

something new
nights
of sleep
the hotel futon
a womb

This Short Life

no one
bothers me
for tips,
at the rickety table
poems come out minimalist

what would it be like?
I ask the Tokyo lamppost
about this newness,
I imagine washing
countless coffee cups

a coffee shop
towel
handed me,
I wipe
these Tokyo eyes

even
these five lines down
slide, slide,
look! so much less
than thirty-one

alone
and still
alone,
I walk in a warm
haze

and so
there's this day
to pass through,
awake I am now
for the passing

This Short Life

am I
on holiday
with this me?
again I write tanka
on my hotel desk

Shinjuku
flares with its
neon,
a solitary sandwich man
with his huge sign of pleasure

how the quiet
settles
me,
I sit before
the weaving board

Sanford Goldstein

having
found
my ordinary life,
calm as I
walk through

everything moves off,
clouds, waves,
faces,
only the empty
remains

shower
relief
along a seaside road,
how the dim April light
makes me calm

This Short Life

the wind
might as well take
these five lines down.
so fleeting.
the infinitesimal fraction of now

so far
to the left of
anguish.
I walk with
these five lines down

tempted
in spite of a diet
I want a spark of body glow.
from the cake shop.
one small white bag

retire
as a baker
of bread?
how I'd love
to maul dough

at last
cleaning out shelves,
cupboards,
in Japan
there's no April Passover

age
also had
its dreams,
they push past
today's now

This Short Life

in the shower
I sing
"Billy Boy"—
how joyous that camp song
sung forty-five years ago

how bright
tonight's light
in the falling snow,
I raise bright images
to calm my desperate hands

to clean
even a closet,
a bedroom floor,
this October light
steadies me

Sanford Goldstein

no lip movement
and still the music
of walk,
a seaside bird
above violent waves

confessions you want?
all right
then!
how cloudy
September's sky

to get
beyond the bare
these fifteen years?
a five-lines-down
immediacy

65

This Short Life

this morning's
November fog
fits my mood,
I sink into a fine shudder
of my body's integrity

to keep
a small segment
intact,
at least this small
morning walk

I want
to tip
my daughter,
she serves sadness
at the waffle shop

highlight
of this cold October
night,
I take my closet bed
and get ready for sleep

the toast
and jam
did their duty,
and newspaper sports
turned all right

I'm that dog
on a short October
leash,
I gut-wail a call
to romp in the sand

This Short Life

everywhere
bright light punches
this me,
on corners before walls,
hands on sliding doors

helping
the crone
lift her baby cart,
I tip my hat
to her socks and rags

trying
before the two guests
arrive,
I put the disorder
into order

Sanford Goldstein

nothing
going for me
this Saturday night,
all day
at the washer-dryer

we dissect
the Shakespearean sonnet
even my students know,
we love that well
what will leave ere long

not quite
Richard Cory
and I click the catalogue,
at the end
tears fall

This Short Life

where's the sad
weaving through
my lines?
just going along
this me in May

exhausted
I watch the sushi
conveyer belt,
I choose
two white fish

want
to select
one special past moment,
its memory never
changed

Sanford Goldstein

a faraway
sky-blue
from my office window,
students on grass
under red maple leaves

a Sado
fisher-woman
arranges her scarf,
in her small net
a broken wedding ring

they hang
the seaweed
with blue clothespins,
the young mother squats,
her baby on her back

This Short Life

my midnight
tanka
quiet,
their music broken
by a next-door baby's cry

her ping pong
ball clicked
at the table's edge,
the sound comes back
at midnight

on the streetcar
home in Nagasaki
I hang on a strap,
two students sad
at the back

Death

Sanford Goldstein

on
the bus strap
sudden the thought,
endings,
I stare out this oriental window

I have lived
by halves
in long separations,
sixteen years
since her death

that white cloth
covering her face
again remembered,
tonight
sixteen years

This Short Life

irreversible
the morning
before,
I see again
her cloth-covered face

sudden
as rain,
as desire,
I see her
cloth-covered face

sixteen years
since her death
though alive in memory:
so vivid that first Tokyo subway,
how her New York know-how got us through

Sanford Goldstein

how soon
memory and
still soon,
never forgotten
that cloth-covered face

with great
relief did that
young bride let go,
she helped the cancer
be victorious

amid
piles of flowers
and downcast faces,
how that young bride
looked content in the casket

This Short Life

young feet
running
along the corridor
to the dying mother's
bedside

one long
morning walk
like a film seen backward,
her death
leading the way

so lively
my uncle
who died,
never did I think the disease
would make him jump

Sanford Goldstein

during
the seven-mile
walk,
the dead came along
this April day

over
a chopstick
lunch,
again a review
of endings

only July tenth
long in advance
of that stark day,
September twenty-second
a long way to go

This Short Life

again
a new October
morning,
I recall the face of my mother,
the face of my aunt

the face
of Caesar
Brutus-stabbed,
tonight's tv
memorial

almost broken,
broken,
chains of connection,
some having died,
some corridor silent

Sanford Goldstein

eating
dinner alone
before the set,
tears gather
for the one gone forever

up the steep
slope
where once we ran,
the long decades up
and down

eighty-eight
is close enough
for death,
and still, still,
a few people say *stay*

81

This Short Life

dizzy I am
as I walk these winter
roads,
one small slip into a ravine
and I'm a goner

an older man
at a year-end party
wants to live,
he says forty more,
much too much for me

pulled one way
by my son,
one by my daughter,
death will take me
before I choose

Sanford Goldstein

my ill English
friend wants to live
and live,
may she go on longer
than this old-man me

how I cried
when my brother's
first wife died,
every now and then
I cry for my dead wife

death
during a long midnight
sleep,
I think
that would be okay

83

This Short Life

to bed
at seven-thirty
is what I want,
longer days too much
for me

Food, Drink

Sanford Goldstein

along
this snow-layered
street,
a bakery shop
oh, this morning relief

how thick
the silence
of those two men,
fingers wedged against
forks, knives

my stomach
swells along
this oriental road,
the bread, the rice,
the chopstick mixture

This Short Life

for lunch
the security of
my office,
the old stand-by
peanut butter and jam

lunch
left in a bag
at the airline counter,
I rush back
to find it gone

the cake
all
devoured,
nothing gained,
nothing lost

Sanford Goldstein

donuts
I devour
this long morning,
their memory
impossible to appease

before my eyes,
métier,
epiphany,
the master chef in long black sleeves
pulls a coup!

again
after twenty-eight
years,
chicken rice
with a spoon

This Short Life

preparing
the Valentine
chocolate,
spoon licks,
marshmallow bites

the call
greeting me
the same,
how bitter the tea
after my reprimand

trying to eliminate
this belly-pain,
I sing some sad ones,
soft my voice
in tonight's shower

Sanford Goldstein

at the Chinese
from behind
my table,
the slurp
of noodles

desire
has to be
cancelled,
ever the widower in old weeds,
I take my coffee black

I have found
a tanka corner
for Japanese tea,
it suits
my blue mood

91

This Short Life

even beer
memories flow
here,
I sit in this study
of my fifty-year-old student

this big
chicken-rice
spoon,
each mouthful
a memory of the dead one

in earlier days
we ate like kids
with spoons, big ones,
how delicious her chicken rice
and candy bars for the movie

is she too
a wraith,
her lips in shadow,
how my coffee cup
is lifted high

tonight's
snack
makes it a holiday,
my kid asks for time off
before the set

my trip begins
a bacon-egg-coffee
reminder,
again I wait
at Niigata station

This Short Life

across
the aisle
chopstick manipulation,
I drink tea
and find the wonder of roof tiles

the other
over coffee
this distant morning,
I list her
among the wraiths

the rickety
coffee table
with cheese cake,
I see its petite fork
and of course a cherry

the coffee house
hang-out,
Japanese smoking in a quiet corner,
music there is
while I write my poem

an offer
at the Shinjuku
coffee shop,
a second cup
without even asking

alone
and hopeless,
helpless,
there's toast and coffee
and the rest

This Short Life

to wake
without stomach
pains,
find there's juice
in the hotel lobby

startled
to find chocolate
with my coffee,
and the waitress
fills my cup again

not a word
between
father and son,
I watch as I drink
my coffee at the shop

fish broiling
on sticks
over charcoal,
my gaijin nose
on this Shinjuku street

at the coffee shop
they study
while they drink and write,
entrance exam day
at Tokyo University

why so grim
that Japanese student
before his father?
their breakfast,
how fast it's devoured

This Short Life

with green tea
I have
Japanese cakes,
two hundred yen
for two

no one
rushes me out
tonight,
I can coffee-shop drink
and spill poems

after
the weaving lesson's
over,
how rich the brown
cup of tea

Sanford Goldstein

at last night's
student party,
I drank three glasses,
these offered by
three tall coeds

how tough
tonight's steak,
and I ponder the latest chew,
was it a piece
of horse?

after the exam
corrections,
coffee and cake,
how slow the long walk
home

This Short Life

devouring
a stupid hamburger
in my office,
time off
between Japanese classes

rain
brings out
the donuts in me,
I buy two
for tonight's snack

this April day
a rhythm
of my own,
morning coffee drunk
while the sun breaks through

Sanford Goldstein

how confident
that young Japanese
with his fork,
dish finished,
he licks his lips

eating
sandwiches
at lunch,
again I give up
being lean, being supple

last snack
readied for
tonight,
it will be diet time
with my kid tomorrow

101

This Short Life

hoist
the beer bottle
in a New Year hand,
pour out
the mutability

something
in the lingering smell
of breakfast toast,
I tighten the brown bag
I carry in the December snow

huddling
in an oriental
coffee shop,
the flow of my poems
cold, stiff

Sanford Goldstein

a winter table
foursome
talking,
spilling their cleverness
over loaded forks

beer poured
into my Chinese
soup bowl,
I am shouted at
drink! drink!

asked
to join the drinking ladder
after the first party,
I decline as usual,
beer's really not for me

This Short Life

I fork
my cake,
I take my coffee black,
another world disaster
on the tube

I shall assume
an Elizabethan
or Meiji cape,
my mind scattering
breakfast crumbs

how cool
last night's
trivialities,
a snack before the set,
funny-face contest with my kid

Sanford Goldstein

I went
through the motions of
alternating sake, beer,
I asked questions
to Japanese hair, Japanese teeth

I remember
parties when students
sang, hummed,
now only exhausted faces
over poured beer

on a square
lacquered dish
I left what I didn't want,
over the eel and rice
my chopsticks pause

This Short Life

exhaustion
on her face
with chopstick lift,
mouth tangled
with foreign words

shrimp
turn orange
in the pan,
I fan
my startled face

I sleep nowadays
though my stomach
keeps caving in,
an empty
empty

feeling
like a gaijin
mispronouncing words,
somehow I get through
and order a small steak

spooning up
the chicken rice
after twenty-eight years,
on that Friday night
spoons and plates were two

even along
the ancient sites
of temple walls,
the garden stones
remind me of bacon and eggs

Zen, God, Faith, Doubt

sad
about the group
he signed into,
he believes in mankind,
not God

again
this Saturday
sadness,
again I say
no God

how useless
is heavenly belief,
so distant,
loose as butter
sputtering in a pan

This Short Life

to have faith,
faith,
and more faith,
so much doubt
in my tearful eyes

today
I picked up
and dropped them off,
so many bundles
of religious regret

said
no God
this morning,
how lonely
the late walk home

the anguish
sits
forever,
oh, this Buddhist
belly

to stir
these lines
into the profound,
I'd have to detour,
to pause and pause

how easy
the faith before
a Shinto shrine,
three palm claps
and a coin toss

This Short Life

how neat
the straw slippers
at the Zen meeting,
they speak
the wordless

when
she was alive,
I couldn't keep up,
my Zen lagged
behind hers

to wake
and know
separation,
no clock
on this Zen wall

Sanford Goldstein

and did
Zen's Seymour
hate the world?
the reason he died
I will never know

often
I feel it's not
for me,
this Zen
world

my own
Buddha goodwill
persists,
this inability
to say no

This Short Life

I should
like for me
his hours,
hours of the Zen master's
confidence

as if
not my shoulder
for the master's stick,
even forty strikes
not enough

koan analysis
leaves me
in doubt,
Zen breathing
does not help

Sanford Goldstein

never
will I know
it,
the sound of
one hand clapping

to leap
through
so appealing,
still, only a
walk-through

staying
at the long Saturday
service,
not once did I feel
God's presence

This Short Life

cameras
keep snapping at
Ryōanji's rocks,
the fifteenth
will never be seen

Hebrew school over
and I run
to my favorite store,
how delicious
the coconut bars look

I asked
my Hebrew school teacher
about food:
could Moses with the manna
ask for lemon pie?

Sanford Goldstein

at elementary school
all sang the Christmas
carols,
a Jewish student told me
to move my lips, not my voice

becoming
a man at thirteen
during my Bar Mitzvah,
somehow I felt
I did not qualify

while I attended synagogue
services at fourteen,
my grandfather never spoke,
his voice box
removed long ago

This Short Life

prayers
said so fast
at the synagogue,
even the English section
too slow for me

in the Army
on Sundays
Jews were called aside,
told to pick up
cigarette butts

long march
with rifle
and full backpack,
the soldier behind trips me,
you killed Christ, he says

Sanford Goldstein

the tall recruit
leaps on my bunk
in desire,
I shout *get off!*
never seen such a Jew, he says

Minimalist Humor

Sanford Goldstein

the old teacher
along the corridor
picking his nose,
he greets me
with a bow

how red
the faces
of my Japanese students,
only a quiz
with one question

a story
I long worked
over,
my satiric laugh,
phony as the brown envelope

This Short Life

even kids
think it's
funny,
my nasal
voice

lo!
there's a gaijin
and another,
this me
I call Japanese

the burp
at the next
table,
how content that Japanese
with his toothpick

only
a Niigata peasant
am I,
Shinjuku
is vast

head
whirling
with taxes,
my list
longer and longer

jumping rope
one hundred times
and I trip,
one thousand's
the center of the universe

This Short Life

all dressed
for the party
at eight,
I stare at the ink spot
on my brown shoes

reading over
my latest
tanka collection,
find the commonplace
still makes me frown

at the party
toast,
I too lift my sake cup,
I manage
a sip

the lazy-susan
whirls
round and round,
five hostesses
walk with elegance

my voice
disintegrates
on "Daisy" —
the end of back-to-back
classes

Shakespeare
calls his fourteen
a miracle,
my own five
somehow got through

This Short Life

standing
resigned
on the crowded bus,
doughnut smell
from my paper bag

my poems
I read
in class,
is it their melody that
puts my students to sleep?

tonight
thoughts about
my distant campus kid,
how she dreams
of a green convertible

Sanford Goldstein

a brooding
silence
on my kid's face,
I ask her
what I did this time

how silent
these Japanese
at their Christmas party,
is this really
the English-Speaking Society?

sometimes,
dear Hamlet,
yes that's how I feel,
buddies are we,
insomniac buddies

This Short Life

not one
acquainted
with the night,
I go to bed
early

a funny face
give-and-take
with my kid,
these stay-at-home days
with her bound ankle

insomnia
numbers
twelve
to
five

even
the bored faces
laugh,
my sudden rage
in class

some samurai
wielding a sword
over a bowed back?
no, the coach
at the afternoon drill

jostled by
bus elbows,
arms bundle-weighted,
as fate
it's not that bad

This Short Life

my kid
turns
regal,
allowing
a cheek-kiss

that bent back
in Greek shorts
jabbing the mule,
doesn't she know
it's Sunday and Mother's Day?

the talk
slides back
and forth,
sometimes on suicide,
sometimes a ride on a ferry

Sanford Goldstein

at last
home from
Star Wars,
I am home
to take down my closet bed

many walk
with dogs
and old men,
two kids
chase a tail

the fraud
in me
nods and nods,
not a word understood
from the flower-master

This Short Life

poor gaijin
Goldstein,
watching, watching—
the Best
of Ten

I read
her e-mail
waiting for my return,
my own,
not her boyfriend's

tourists
clicking
their cameras,
they like the way
tea's whisked at the ceremony

in the bright
end-of-May
light,
I see age
crawling down my chin

his
peck
at her cheek,
is the three-week separation
a turn-off-the-light kiss?

Minimalist Multitudes

was it
her precious voice
in my dream
whispering
in the cold?

arousal
for a brief
street moment,
up a stair
and the mediocre returns

leaping from my cart
last night's oil fell
scouring the tile
the green peas landed
on my cast-off boot

This Short Life

all night
cold bones
cold mind,
spring corners
thick with snow

hearing
Obama on
tape,
I remember Kennedy,
I remember Thanksgiving

the page fills
with red scrawls
of poetry,
they crowd into
commonplace corners

loaded
with chocolate,
donuts and stuff,
I prepare
to confront tonight's loneliness

facing
the dissolving
night,
all connections
severed

how easy
one fills gaps
in life,
the divorced, the dead,
and this me

This Short Life

I move
in a cul-de-sac
world,
the same routes,
holes in every turn

it's work
at my desk,
a glance outside,
a falling
white wind

after the dinner
I walk
to the bus,
dark and narrow
this stretch of road

again
the affair
falters,
all paths
lead home

the ten p.m. bus
and its exhausted
load,
we pass
empty stops

letters
written light
as white feathers,
I cover multitudes
of omissions

This Short Life

no relief
can be found
anywhere,
a permanent wedge
on which to place a hat

out of step
am I with
today's chemistry,
the compounds I seek
nowhere found

tanka,
your weight
does its damage,
even the delicate line
of snow on pine scatters

the final
chill this Niigata
day,
the envelope with
its rejection slip

sister
recovering
in the hospital,
my mother with flu,
my kid's appendix scar

her voice
like fragile
threads,
the bright needle
in her hand

This Short Life

it's useless
I know
and still, still,
these five
lines down

classes
lifted from my Western
back,
I feel lighter
on this oriental bridge

how white
the water was
last night,
no wine for me
at the Italian

Sanford Goldstein

to have faith
faith
and more faith,
I find envy
in my this-world eye

I stick out
my red tongue
and batter my hat,
I want, you know,
a February laugh

he called
for a battering
of the heart—
and he was right,
was ripe for blows

This Short Life

at the crucial
moment,
my sleeves rebelled,
pulled away
and left

a bus trip
wind-hurling
and pulling
the February dark
against my eyes

something
wedged in today's
wind,
I think of my mother
across the ocean

shadows
on the screen
moving to rhythm,
I close my eyes
to shut out the lack

could I
Emily Dickinson
my way though,
what splendid colors
might the world assume

two sisters
violent in their opposition
to work —
and this tanka world
made lonelier

This Short Life

liquid black
those pupils
of a bus kid
staring, staring
on his mother's lap

round a curve
or even a sharp angle,
pebbles in my shoes,
I stumble
and this avalanche sky

I'm old, old,
she says
as if ready to cave in
this desire
for her early final

Sanford Goldstein

analysis
walks
with me
even as I count,
breathe

Afterword

I have been an admirer of the tanka of Sanford Goldstein for as long as I have been reading tanka in English. A professor in the United States and Japan, translator (with his professional partners) of scores of classics of modern Japanese literature, and a skilled editor and poet in his own right, Goldstein is the grand old man of tanka in English. Unfailingly helpful to me and other poets, he is the author of cogent critiques, and in spite of advancing age and the debilities that come with it, a gifted poet who continues to compose poetry. It is a pleasure and a privilege to assist him in the publication of this book.

Goldstein's tanka are distinguished by an honesty that is rare in literature, but lacking in bitterness, cynicism or irony. His tanka are artless; they seem like plain speaking, but the adroitness of his chosen details and the validity of his insights raise the persona of his poems to the status of an Everyman. He is not just Sanford Goldstein, poet, professor, and father; he is all of us.

Ranging from about ten to twenty syllables in length, the tanka in this collection are typical of Goldstein's work. Minimalism persists throughout forty years, beginning in 1977 with *This Tanka World*, and continuing to this day. Yet he has also written full-

bodied tanka, hypermetric lines, and experimented
with the short-long-short-long-long format. Never
dogmatic, he chooses what works best for any given
poem.

> the cat
> like something
> out of Noh,
> so delicate its footsteps
> in an autumn field

We've all seen a cat walking softly on the Earth,
but how many of us have seen a Noh dancer in it? Yet
once the comparison is made, the slow dignified glide
of cat and dancer is irresistible. Commonplace things
are made splendid by the master's pen.

> during
> the seven-mile
> walk,
> the dead came along
> this April day

Even now, at eighty-eight, Goldstein continues to
walk an hour a day. He meets his neighbors, stray
dogs, and the ghosts of the dead when he does.
Already a widower, he has lost other relatives lately.

under
my 11 p.m.
shower,
the white soap streaks
reciting my list of the dead

Being Jewish, he has lost more than most of us:
the soap streaks in the shower cannot help but send a
frisson down our spines. Such simple things. Such
unspeakable things, yet there they are. Critics have
complained that tanka are too small to address serious
topics, but what could be more serious than the
Holocaust? It is tanka's ability to evoke far more than
it says that makes it a fitting tool for whatever subject
is brought to it, and Goldstein is its master.

the Chinese tea
warms,
settles,
outside
a quiet snow

Goldstein's spiritual practice—his Zen, his
Judaism, his sensitivity—make meaning from the most
ordinary of things. He is ever mindful of what he
experiences and puts it down in words. Although
many writers of Japanese-style poetry make overt
Orientalist references, Goldstein does not. He lives in

Japan, so his Oriental motifs are the world in which he actually lives, not an exotic Other.

When Goldstein published his previous book, *Journeys Far and Near*, he thought it would be his last, but I knew that all of his tanka had not yet been published. When he mentioned the minimalist tanka in an old notebook, I told him I would be pleased to publish it. He demurred at first—trouble with his health makes working on a book increasingly difficult —but eventually he decided he liked the project enough to give it a go. My labor has been to correct errors (very rare in the work of an English professor) and to make suggestions regarding scope and approach.

I see age taking its toll on him. I have had to remind him of matters already discussed and settled, to resend emails he has lost, and to help him keep track of where we are in the process. Other times, I find emails as meticulous as only an English professor can be, pointing out an overlooked comma or with commentary on famous Minimalist poets. The brilliant mind remains.

In light of his advancing age and illness, *This Short Life* is an especially poignant memento of the fragility of life. In truth, we never know when we go to bed at night if we will wake up in the morning. We never take a step knowing if we will be able to continue walking. We never accomplish anything without the risk that we may never complete what we start. The very short poems of *This Short Life* are as ephemeral and immediate as the moments they capture. It requires a man of almost ninety to show us just how brief and perishable our lives are.

Whether Sandy will be able to produce another book, I don't know. I know that he keeps writing, and he still has old notebooks with tanka that he hasn't published. I will continue to encourage him to submit work for publication as long as he has the energy to do so. I will hope for more, but in this short life, who can ever be certain?

M. Kei
Perryville, Maryland, USA
1 January 2014

Biographies

Born in 1925 and now 88, Sanford Goldstein has written many books of tanka, including *This Tanka World*, his first book in 1977. His latest book before *This Short Life* was *Journeys Far and Near : tanka roads* (Inkling Press 2013). His other works include short stories, essays, co-translations of famous Japanese tanka writers, including *Tangled Hair* by Akiko Yosano (1971) and Takuboku Ishikawa's *Romaji Diary and Sad Toys* (1985) (these translations with Seishi Shinoda). He has published minimalist poems off and on, but this present book is his first major work to focus on Minimalist poetry.

Kazuaki Wakui is an artist, essayist, photographer, and cartoonist of manga (Japanese-style humour).

M. Kei is a tall ship sailor and award-winning poet who lives on Maryland's Eastern shore. He was the editor-in-chief of *Take Five : Best Contemporary Tanka*, *Vols. 1–4*, the editor of *Bright Stars, An Organic Tanka Anthology*; and the editor of *Atlas Poetica : A Journal of Poetry of Place in Contemporary Tanka*. His most recent collection of poetry is *January; A Tanka Diary.*

Praise for This Short Life

Sanford Goldstein is known worldwide for his emotionally robust tanka, written in his distinctive "spilling" style. This collection of shorter poems at the "minimalist" end of the spectrum demonstrates his ability to surprise and delight us from inside what may appear to be another persona, but what is in fact classic Goldstein in timbre of voice, subject matter, and resilient spirit. His achievements in English-language tanka claim yet another territory. These poems are variously mobile and pungent, light and arrow-swift, and a joy to have at this juncture in a long, productive career.

Michael McClintock
President and co-founder, United Haiku and Tanka Society; Lead editor, *The Tanka Anthology* (Red Moon Press, 2003)

The poems in Sanford Goldstein's latest book spring mostly from a rush of writing one particular year in a minimalist way, seemingly more by accident than intent. The results may not always seem minimalistic, but they are in Goldstein's view, but more in comparison to the nonsyllabic short-long-short-long-long form, which he says he prefers, than to a 5-7-5-7-7 syllabic form. The book's title, *This Short Life*, is a reference not just to how short his long life seems, but how his life has been filled with short poetry. Goldstein, of course, is one of tanka's greatest masters in English, and these minimalist tanka show one of the reasons why. Treat yourself to these revealing poems by reading them slowly.

Michael Dylan Welch
Tanka Society of America founder

Sanford thought that *Journeys Far and Near*—his recent collection—would be his last published book. He didn't count on M. Kei being wise enough to know there were far more tanka to be published. I'm guessing, and hoping, that even this present book will not be his last; the old man still has so much to say.

He can still write tanka like no one else. Tanka which seem simple but hold deep truths. Tanka that seem complex but go straight to the heart of things.

Joy McCall
Author of *circling smoke, scattered bones*

Made in the USA
Charleston, SC
09 March 2014